HERE COMES

THE

BRIDE

Jewish Wedding Customs
And The Messiah

RICHARD BOOKER

Here Comes the Bride

Printed in the United States of America

ISBN 0-9615302-4-3

Cover Design by Michael Washer

Table of Contents

Preface

In the fourth century, a man named John Chrysostom (344 A.D.-407 A.D.) was the bishop of the Church of Antioch. He was a great orator. In fact his name means, "Golden-Mouthed." He had tremendous influence and is considered one of the greatest of the early church Fathers.

But John Chrysostom had a problem - he hated Jews. He blamed the entire Jewish race for the death of Jesus and sought to separate Christianity from its Jewish roots.

John Chrysostom gave a series of eight sermons in which he spoke violently against the Jews. His sermons were put in written form and widely circulated. Although many early church Fathers spoke harshly against the Jews, John Chrysotom was the most vicious. His sermons fanned the flames of anti-Semitism that became the official teaching and practice of the church for the next 1,600 years.

The *Jewish-Christian Relations Series* was written to refute and rebuke the writings of John Chrysostom. It was written to express love to the Jewish people, to call the church to repentance for its anti-Semitic past and to help the church understand God's eternal purposes for the Jewish people and the nation of Israel.

The sermons given by John Chrysostom began a legacy of hate towards the Jewish people that is still with us today. *The Jewish-Christian Relations Series* was written with the hope that it will cause a new beginning of love and understanding between Christians and Jews.

You may order additional copies of this booklet and other relevant materials by using the Order Form in the back of this publication. SHALOM!

HERE COMES THE BRIDE

Jewish Wedding Customs and the Messiah

One of the most beautiful pictures of God's love for us is the ancient Jewish wedding. It consisted of three phases: the betrothal phase, the wedding phase and the celebration phase.

Everyone loves a wedding, except dad when he's paying the bills. Weddings are joyous occasions that fill us with hope and promise for the future of the bride and bridegroom. Let's spend the next few minutes together while I tell you about the Jewish wedding and the hope and promise of redemption it portrays.

The Marriage Covenant

In the ancient pagan world, when a man wanted to marry a woman he took her to his house and had intercourse with her and she became his wife. There was no formal public ceremony in front of witnesses to "tie the knot." There was no family support. There was no agreement on the relationship. There was no permanence or protection for the woman, nor the marriage.

The man could put away the woman and marry someone else simply by the act of sex. I think we can all agree that something as important as marriage and family needs to be based on more than feelings and sex.

When God revealed Himself to the Jews, He gave them specific instructions for marriage in order to sanctify it properly as the basic unit of society. He wanted to give marriage and family the permanency, protection and moral framework it needed for the good of society and the established social order.

His instructions for marriage required the man to actually "acquire" a wife publicly in the presence of witnesses. This was to be a formal process that would give sanctity to the relationship. God intended the marriage relationship to be permanent for the good of the couple and society as a whole.

God recognized our human weaknesses and allowed for divorce, if the bride was not a virgin or when there was infidelity. We read in Deuteronomy, *"When a man takes (acquires) a wife and marries her, and it happens that she finds no favor in his eyes because he has found some uncleanness in her (not a virgin), and he writes her a certificate of divorce, puts it in her hand, and sends her out of his house" (Deut. 24:1).*

This formal process of marriage led to various customs among the Jewish people. When a young Jewish man "set his eyes" on a young Jewish woman he asks for her hand in marriage by means of a *marriage contract*. This contract was actually a covenant *(brit* in Hebrew).

Many times the father chose the bride for the son and decided the terms of the contract. The father might also use the services of a matchmaker. The matchmaker (*shadkhan* in Hebrew) was the expert in finding just the right bride for the father's son. He often held the key to the success of the marriage and had to be a person of the highest character and integrity.

As just mentioned, the marriage contract was actually a covenant. In ancient times, a covenant was considered to be a legal binding agreement between parties.

One particular type of covenant was a blood covenant. A blood covenant was a sacred agreement between two parties by which they committed their lives to one another. They pledged their relationship by killing an animal and making a sacrifice.

The God of the Hebrews considered marriage to be a blood covenant. In fact, when God spoke of His relationship to the Jewish people, He did so in terms of a blood covenant.

From God's perspective, He married the Hebrews in the sense that He committed His life to them by covenant, as they did to Him. God acquired them for Himself through the marriage covenant.

We read these words from God, "Gather My saints together to Me, those who have made a covenant with Me by sacrifice"(Ps. 50:15).

From God's point of view, marriage was a sacred blood covenant where two people mutually committed their lives to each other. This is why God, at one time, chastised the Jewish priests for divorcing their wives.

The prophet Malachi said the Jews were "breaking their commitment to their wives by covenant"(See Mal. 2:14).

The Betrothal Phase

The first phase of the Jewish wedding is the betrothal (*Shitre Erusin* in Hebrew). The young man prepares a marriage contract or covenant which he presents to the young woman and her father. The Hebrew word for this marriage contract is *Ketubah.* It is a formal written document which stipulates the terms of the marriage proposal he is making. He probably goes over the contract with his father to make sure Abba is in agreement. He then goes to the house where the young woman lives and makes the proposal to her and her father.

The Bride Price

The most important part of the proposal is the *bride price.* This is the price the young man is willing to pay the father for the father's permission for the young man to marry his daughter. This might seem strange to us today, but we have to put ourselves in their culture to understand this practice.

In times past when people lived on the farm, life was hard. Physical labor was hard. They didn't live in a push-button society with all the creature comforts we take for granted today. Although a daughter could steal her daddy's heart, she was considered somewhat of a financial burden to him because she couldn't do her share of the hard work. Sons were considered more valuable simply because they were able to "help carry the load."

The bride price is high as a means of compensating the family for the financial liability of raising a daughter as well as being an expression of the young man's love for his hoped-for bride.

The Cup of Acceptance

If the marriage contract and the bride price are acceptable to the father, the young man would pour a *cup of wine* for his beloved and wait nervously to see if she will drink it.

This cup of wine represents the blood covenant commitment and union they would have as husband and wife. It is the young man's way of "popping the question" to her. If she drinks the cup, this shows her acceptance of the marriage proposal. This was her "yes" to the proposal.

The bridegroom prepares for this joyous occasion by bringing *gifts* for his beloved. They were a token of his love and a constant reminder to the bride that she is his special treasure. She, in turn, treasures him and his gifts and makes good use of them as she waits for the time they can be together as husband and wife.

After her young man leaves, and before their wedding, the bride takes a special bath as part of a ceremonial cleansing to prepare herself for the days ahead. The Hebrew word for this ceremonial cleansing is *Mikveh.* It is a washing or cleansing that denotes a purifying through baptism.

At this point the young couple are betrothed. This means they are legally married, although they are not yet ready or able to live together as husband and wife. The marriage is consummated later in the celebration phase. The nearest we have to this in the West is the engagement period.

The Wedding Chamber

Before leaving the house of his newly betrothed, the eager young man announces to her that he is *going to prepare a place for her*. But as soon as it is prepared, he will come again for her. They will not see each other until he comes for her. This long period of separation will be hard but definitely worth the wait.

The bridegroom then returns home and starts preparing a place for he and his bride to honeymoon. This is usually a room he builds onto his father's house. In Jewish weddings, the *chuppah* represents this wedding chamber. He wants to make the honeymoon suite as nice as he can. But he is also in a hurry to finish so he can go get his bride.

It might take a full year or more to complete the bridal chamber. Naturally the eager bridegroom works as fast as he can and is tempted to "cut corners." So it is left to his father to decide when the place is ready. We can certainly see the wisdom here. If someone asks the young man the date of his wedding, he would reply, "I don't know, only my father knows."

Making Herself Ready

While the bridegroom is busy preparing a place, the bride is busy preparing *herself*. She would use the gifts her bridegroom has given her to make herself beautiful. Of course, she does not use her gifts for selfish purposes but for the benefit of her beloved.

Although she does not know when he will come for her, she wants to look her best. She reorders her entire life to make herself ready for his coming.

As we can imagine, preparing herself for his coming is the focus and priority of her life. Everything else revolves around this. Her every thought is waiting for the day when she will see him face to face.

When the young bride leaves her house, she wears a veil to let other young men know she is "spoken for." She is no longer available because she has been *bought with a price*.

She is set apart and consecrated to her bridegroom. She will resist any other offers as she waits for her one true love who has bought and paid for her.

The young bride belongs to the one who paid the bride price for her. She is his and his alone. In Hebrew, she is called a *me'kudeshet*, meaning one who is betrothed, sanctified, dedicated to another.

Her veil is a constant reminder to herself and to others that she is betrothed to one who is preparing a place for her where they will enter into the joys of their covenant relationship through marriage.

The Wedding Phase

To the young couple pledged to one another, it seems like an eternity before they will be together. But sure enough, the time comes when the bridegroom's father gives his final inspection approval to the wedding chamber. He then tells his son to go get his bride.

The young man has been eagerly awaiting this word from his father. It doesn't take him long to make his way to his bride's house.

Sometimes the bridegroom would "steal away" his bride like a thief in the night and take her to the wedding chamber.

How exciting and romantic this is for the bride as she waits for her betrothed to come and take her away. *But she never knows when he is coming for her.* She knows he must be about through preparing a place for her, but she doesn't know exactly when he will come. She has to be ready at all times.

If the bridegroom came for his bride in the middle of the night, the bride made special preparations for his coming. She had to be ready to go at a moment's notice.

It was the custom for the bride to keep an oil lamp beside her bed, along with her veil and other belongings. Her bridesmaids are also waiting making sure they have plenty of oil for their lamps.

The time of waiting is about over as the big day is near. The bride and the bridegroom have made their preparations and will soon be one.

Coming for the Bride

The day of the actual wedding has come and the bridegroom, accompanied by his close friends, makes his way to the bride's house.

The anxious bridegroom wants to surprise his bride but also needs to give her a warning so she can be ready to go with him. She has to light her lamp, "put on her face" and get her things. No time for packing!

When the wedding party gets close to the house, they *give a shout* and blow the shofar (ram's horn) to let the bride know her bridegroom is coming.

This is the moment for which they have both been waiting. She's awake and alert and waiting! He's in a hurry! When they arrive, the bridegroom and his friends charge right into the house and carry off the bride and her maids.

Now wedding parties can be noisy. As the young people make their way through the dark streets, lamps aglow and voices loud, they awake the neighbors who realize a wedding party is taking place.

Neighbors are naturally curious. They peek out the windows to see the identity of the bride, but she's wearing her veil.

At this point the neighbors don't know who the bride is, but she will be returning in a week with her veil removed. Then everyone will know the identity of the bride. Some will be surprised, but others will have guessed it all along.

Consummating the Marriage

When the wedding party arrives at the house of the bridegroom's father, the newly weds go into the wedding chamber for a seven day honeymoon. Here they *consummate the marriage* and establish their covenant union. When the young couple have intercourse, the bride's hymen is broken and blood is spilled to show she was a true virgin. The blood covenant of marriage has now been sealed.

The groom's best friend stands outside the room near the door waiting for the groom to tell him the marriage is complete.

At the appropriate moment, the new husband takes the honeymoon sheet stained with blood and gives it to his friend. This special friend then presents the blood-stained sheet to those gathered to celebrate as the evidence that the two have become one.

The Celebration Phase

The celebration lasts for seven days. While the newly weds are inside the wedding chamber honeymooning, the invited guest are outside having a party. They celebrate for seven days until the newly weds emerge from their wedding chamber.

When the new couple make their appearance, the guest clap and cheer and congratulate them. There is a lot of singing and dancing. It's all very festive. This is followed by a joyous feast called the *marriage supper* which is given to honor the new husband and wife.

When the party is over, the bride and groom depart for their own house where they will live together in wedded bliss, and sometimes not so much bliss. Now that the bride is married, she has discarded her veil. As they make their way back through the same streets they were on seven days earlier, the neighbors are now able to know the identity of the bride. They too rejoice and celebrate the marriage covenant that God established in the young couple's lives.

God Takes a Bride

As previously mentioned, when God revealed Himself to the Hebrews, He chose to relate to them through marriage by means of a covenant.

God would acquire Israel as His bride. God was His own shadkhan. He chose Abraham and his descendants simply because that was His plan and purpose. He is the perfect matchmaker. He would be their heavenly husband and lover of their soul.

When God delivered the Hebrews from Egypt, He said to them, *"I will bring you out ... I will rescue you ... I will redeem you ... I will take you as My people, and I will be your God ... "(Ex. 6:6-7).*

God is using marriage talk when He says He will "take" the Hebrews. He will acquire them as His bride.

God spoke these words to His bride through the prophet Isaiah, *"For your Maker is your husband, the*

LORD of Hosts is His name; and your Redeemer is the Holy One of Israel; He is called the God of the whole earth.

"For the LORD has called you like a woman forsaken and grieved in spirit, like a youthful wife when you were refused, says your God"(Is. 54:5-6)

God clearly states He is in a marriage covenant relationship with Israel as His wife.

God then added these words through Ezekiel, *"... Yes, I swore an oath to you and entered into covenant with you, and you became Mine, says the Lord God"(Ezek. 16:8).*

God's Marriage Contract

When God acquired Israel as His bride, He offered her a formal, written marriage contract. The marriage contract or covenant is recorded in the book of Exodus and continues on for the first five books of the Bible. Here God spells out in detail the terms of the covenant. Since He is the Father of creation, these are the terms which are acceptable to Him. We know this marriage contract (Ketubah) by the name of *Torah*, God's instructions for the marriage agreement.

Since this was to be a marriage contract, the very heart of it required Israel to reject the gods of the pagans and worship only Him. In fact the very first term in the marriage contract was, *"You shall have no other gods before Me"(Ex. 20:3).* God was going to betroth the Hebrews to Himself. They were to be His "me'kudeshet."

God amplified this most basic term of the agreement with these words, *"Hear, O Israel: The LORD our God, the LORD is one! You shall love the LORD your God with all your heart, with all your soul, and with all your strength"(Duet. 6:4-5).*

What a wonderful, loving husband God would be to His bride, Israel. But as with any husband, God would be jealous over His new bride. He said to her, *"For the LORD your God is a consuming fire, a jealous God"(Deut. 4:24).*

If the Hebrews went back to worshipping other gods, God would consider their actions spiritual adultery and the contract would be broken, not by God, but by His unfaithful bride. Instead of receiving their husband God's blessings, they would be cursed. Moses recorded these blessings and curses in Deuteronomy 28. God's bride would lose her national identity, be scattered from her land and miss her Messiah.

Blessings and curses are the norm in any husband-wife relationship. When the bridegroom and bride are faithful to each other, their relationship is blessed. But if one is unfaithful, the relationship is cursed. God would have the same relationship with His bride — Israel.

The Bride Price

When God acquired Israel as His bride, He offered His own bride price. The bride price God paid to purchase Israel was *blood.* He would give the blood of the Passover lamb as the means to bring them, rescue them, redeem them and take them to Himself. His word of comfort to His bride was, *"Now the blood shall be a sign for you on the houses where you are. And when I see the blood, I will pass over you; and the plague shall not be on you to destroy you when I strike the land of Egypt.*

" So this day shall be to you a memorial; and you shall keep it as a feast to the LORD throughout your generations. You shall keep it as a feast by everlasting ordinance"(Ex. 12:13-14).

God then told the Hebrews, that if they accepted the terms of the covenant, He would consider them His special treasure above all the people on the face of the earth.

Exodus 19 reads, *"Now therefore, if you will indeed obey My voice and keep My covenant, then you shall be a special treasure to Me above all people; for all the earth is Mine (Ex. 19:5).*

The Hebrew word for special treasure is *segulah.* It was used by kings to identify certain objects in their possession that meant more to them than all the others.

Although kings valued all their possessions, their special treasures were the most dear to their heart. Whereas men value things, God said that Israel, His bride, would be His most valued treasure.

Any husband should certainly feel this way about his bride. He may have many possessions, but his bride is the most treasured of all that he has.

Likewise, although God loves all of His creation, He especially cares for His bride. She is the object of His love and attention.

The Cup of Acceptance

The Bible tells us that Israel accepted God's marriage contract. We read from Exodus, *"So Moses came and called for the elders of the people, and laid before them all these words which the LORD commanded them. Then all the people answered together and said, 'All that the LORD has spoken we will do.' So Moses brought back the words of the people to the LORD" (Exodus 19:7-8).*

Israel would drink the cup of wine at the Passover covenant meal to show that she accepted God's terms of the marriage contract.

In modern times, the Jewish people drink four cups of wine at the Passover meal. The four cups of wine correspond to the four promises God made to His bride in Exodus 6:6-7. The fourth cup is the marriage covenant cup. When the Jewish people drink it, they are saying "yes" to God's marriage proposal. They may or may not realize the significance of this fourth cup, but God does.

God promised many gifts or blessings to His dearly betrothed Israel. They primarily related to giving her a land flowing with milk and honey, establishing her as the head of the nations, and making a new covenant with her through the Messiah, the Promised Seed of Abraham.

God's promises and blessings to the Hebrew people were everlasting because the marriage covenant He was making with them was everlasting.

Although the Hebrews would fail God many times, God would be faithful to His covenant.

Making Herself Ready

Now that Israel is betrothed to God, she cleanses herself with a mikveh, according to God's instructions. Exodus reads, "*Then the LORD said to Moses, 'Go to the people and consecrate them today and tomorrow, and let them wash their clothes' "(Ex. 19:10).*

God instructed His new bride on how to worship Him and serve Him. He gave her religious instructions that included a tabernacle where He would dwell in her midst, a sacrifice system for her atonement and a priesthood for her representation before Him.

God gave her moral instructions for her purity and sanctification. He gave her civil instructions so she could live as a nation under the righteous government of God. He gave her all the instructions she needed to live as the kind of bride He desired.

The Torah (instructions) that God gave to His bride was her veil. As Israel worshipped God and lived out the terms of the marriage contract, the pagan world would see that Israel had been set apart as the bride of God. She was God's "me'kudeshet."

God's bride had been bought with a price. She belonged to Him and Him alone. She was to have no other lovers but God.

God explained it this way in the book of Leviticus, *"For I am the LORD who brings you up out of the land of Egypt, to be your God. You shall therefore be holy, for I am holy"(Lev. 11:45).*

God's Wedding Chamber

God also prepared a wedding chamber for His bride. That wedding chamber was the *Sabbath.* The Sabbath was the day God gave for His bride to spend time with Him. She was to put aside the cares and chores of the world and spend the day in intimate fellowship with her husband God. Exodus reads, *"Remember the Sabbath day to keep it holy"(Ex. 19:8).*

The word Sabbath means rest. This was the one day of the week God's bride was to rest from her labors and her everyday activities. She was to shut herself in with God and enjoy Him as the bridegroom and bride come to know each other in the wedding chamber.

Once again we read in Exodus, *"Speak also to the children of Israel saying: 'Surely My Sabbaths you shall keep, for it is a sign between Me and you throughout your generations, that you may know that I am the LORD who sanctifies you' "(Ex. 31:13).*

God's Wedding Celebration

God also gave instructions for the wedding celebrations. We call these celebrations the *feasts of the Lord.* Three times a year the males were required to go to Jerusalem for a glorious celebration of their marriage covenant with God.

Passover was the Spring festival celebrating her redemption and deliverance from Egypt. Pentecost was the

Summer festival celebrating her receiving the Torah. Tabernacles was the Fall festival celebrating the end of the harvest season and the coming of the Messiah. These were times of great rejoicing when the people would leave their problems behind and enjoy the presence of God in their midst.

A Tragic Marriage

Unfortunately, God and His new bride did not have a very good marriage. Right after Israel was betrothed, she made a golden calf and worshipped it (Exodus 32). Moses pleaded with God not to destroy Israel. God agreed to the request from Moses but three thousand died as a result of their harlotry.

When God told Israel to go in and posses the land He had given her, she failed to trust God to help her defeat the enemy. As a result, she wandered forty years in the desert. God was merciful to His bride and met all her needs until that rebellious generation died.

After Moses died, Joshua led the people into the promised land. As long as Joshua and the elders who served with him were alive, the people were outwardly faithful to God (Josh. 24:31). But afterwards, they begin to worship the heathen gods and live immorally.

Under the godly leadership of Samuel and King David, Israel was a faithful bride. But for most of the marriage, Israel played the harlot. King Solomon brought disaster on the nation. He took many foreign wives who led him and the nation into idol worship from which they never recovered.

God sent many prophets to warn His bride. But except for a godly remnant, she would not listen. Jeremiah reads, *"I have also sent to you all My servants the prophets, rising up early and sending them, saying, 'Turn now everyone from his evil way, amend your doings, and do not go after other gods to serve them; then you will dwell in the land which I have given you and your fathers.' But you have not inclined your ear, nor obeyed Me" (Jer. 35:15).*

God continued to plead with His bride, but she would not listen. God spoke through Jeremiah, *"They say, if a man divorces his wife, and she goes from him and becomes another man's, may he return to her again'? Would not that land be greatly polluted? But you have played the harlot with many lovers; yet return to Me, says the LORD" (Jer. 3:1).*

Finally, God had no choice but to issue a certificate of divorce. Jeremiah reads, *"Then I saw that for all the causes for which backsliding Israel had committed adultery, I had put her away and given her a certificate of divorce; yet her treacherous sister Judah did not fear, but went and played the harlot. So it came to pass, through her casual harlotry, that she defiled the land and committed adultery with stones and trees. And yet for this all her treacherous sister Judah has not turned to Me with her whole heart, but in pretense, says the LORD" (Jer. 3:8-10).*

We read the following grievous words from Ezekiel, *"But you trusted in your own beauty, played the harlot because of your fame, and poured out your harlotry on everyone passing by who would have it. ... You are an adulterous wife, who takes strangers instead of her husband. ... And I will judge you as women who break wedlock or shed blood are judged; I will bring blood upon you in fury and jealousy. ... For thus says the LORD God; 'I will deal with you as you have done, who despised the oath by breaking the covenant"(Ezek. 16:15,32,38,59).*

A Forgiving Bridegroom

In spite of the fact that God had to divorce His bride, it would be only a temporary separation. For God is a forgiving bridegroom. He promised His wayward bride that He would draw her back to Himself. This is the story of the book of Hosea.

Hosea was a prophet of the LORD. God used his marriage as a visual aid of the tragic marriage God had with Israel. Hosea's wife, Gomer, was a prostitute. She bore Hosea three children. God had Hosea give the children names that reflected His divorce of Israel. Their names were, "God will Scatter," "No Mercy," and "Not My People" Today, this would be like a husband telling his wife to pack her bags and leave the house.

Hosea suffered the humiliation and pain of a wayward wife. Yet he still loved her. She was apart from him and ended up at the public slave market, stripped naked, to be sold to the highest bidder. Hosea humbled himself, went to the slave market and bought his own wife under those conditions. With Hosea's persistent love, Gomer finally repented from her sinful ways and realized she belonged only to Hosea.

God had suffered the humiliation and pain of His wayward wife, Israel. He had to divorce her. Yet, He still loves her. Even though Israel would be far away from her heavenly husband, God would not forsake her. He promised to draw her back to Himself. Israel would finally repent from her wayward ways and return to her God.

During this time of separation from God, Israel would be scattered among the nations. But they would return to their land and their God at the end of the age when the Messiah would come and prepare a festive marriage feast for His bride.

Hosea explains, *"For the children of Israel shall abide many days without king or prince, without sacrifice or sacred pillar, without ephod or teraphim. Afterward the children of Israel shall return and seek the LORD their God and David their king. They shall fear the LORD and His goodness in the latter days (Hos. 3:4-5).*

God gave Israel these words of comfort and assurance, *" 'And it shall be in that day,' says the LORD, that you will call Me 'My Husband,' and no longer call Me 'My Master,' ... I will betroth you to Me forever; Yes, I will betroth you to Me in righteousness and justice, in lovingkindness and mercy, I will betroth you to me in faithfulness, and you shall know the LORD"(Hos. 2:16,19-20).*

What a loving God is this God of the Hebrews!

When God says He will betroth Israel, He means He will take her back as a virgin bride just as if she had never sinned. He will forgive all her wayward ways. This time the marriage will last forever. It will be a marriage characterized by righteousness, justice, lovingkindness, mecy and faithfulness. Israel will know her God and rejoice in their covenant marriage.

Ezekiel adds, *"Nevertheless I will remember My covenant with you in the days of your youth, and I will establish an everlasting covenant with you. And I will establish My covenant with you. Then you shall know that I am the LORD" (Ezek. 16:60,62).*

A New Covenant Marriage

Jeremiah explained that this would be a new covenant God would make with His people, *"Behold, the days are coming, says the LORD, when I will make a new covenant with the house of Israel and with the house of Judah—not according to the covenant that I made with their fathers in the day that I took them by the hand to lead them out of the land of Egypt, My covenant which they broke, though I was a husband to them, says the LORD.*

"But this is the covenant that I will make with the house of Israel after those days, says the LORD: I will put My law in their minds, and write it on their hearts; and I will be their God, and they shall be My people. No more shall every man teach his neighbor, and every man his brother, saying 'know the LORD,' for they all shall know

Me, from the least of them to the greatest of them, says the LORD. For I will forgive their iniquity, and their sin I will remember no more" (Jer. 31:31-34).

Until this marriage is renewed in the latter days, God would call a people out from among the Goyim (Gentiles) who would become part of the bride with Israel.

Isaiah wrote: *"And in that day there shall be a root of Jesse, Who shall stand as a banner to the people; for the Gentiles shall seek Him, and His resting place shall be glorious"(Is. 11:10).*

Jeremiah proclaimed, *"O LORD my strength and my fortress, my refuge in the day of affliction, the Gentiles shall come to You from the ends of the earth and say, 'Surely our fathers have inherited lies, worthless and unprofitable things.' Will a man make gods for himself, which are not gods? Therefore behold, I will this once cause them to know, I will cause them to know My hand and My might; and they shall know that My name is the LORD"(Jer. 16. 19-21).*

Isaiah also wrote, *"I will give you as a light to the Gentiles, that You should be My salvation to the ends of the earth"(Is. 49:6).*

The Messiah Bridegroom

The New Testament presents Yeshua (Jesus) as the fulfillment of God's promise of a new covenant to the Jewish people and a light to the Gentiles. He is the Jewish Redeemer and Savior of the Gentiles.

When Yeshua was presented at the Temple according to the law of Moses, a devout old man named Simeon was there. God had promised him he would not die before he saw the Messiah.

The Spirit of God led Simeon to Yeshua. He took Yeshua in his arms and blessed God and said: *"Lord, now You are letting your servant depart in peace, according to Your word; for my eyes have seen Your salvation which You have prepared before the face of all peoples, a light to bring revelation to the Gentiles, and the glory of Your people Israel"(Luke 2:29-32).*

Mattityahu (Matthew) said that Yeshua fulfilled the following prophecy of Isaiah, "*Behold! My Servant whom I have chosen, My Beloved in whom My soul is well pleased! I have put My Spirit upon Him, and He will declare justice to the Gentiles.*

"He will not quarrel nor cry out, nor will anyone hear His voice in the streets. A bruised reed He will not break, and smoking flax He will not quench, till He sends forth justice to victory; and in His name Gentiles will trust"(Matt. 12:18-21).

They called Yeshua "Immanuel," which means God is with us (Matt. 1:23). God, in the person of Yeshua, came to the house of His bride (eretz Israel - the land of Israel) to present His marriage contract. That marriage contract was the new covenant of which the prophets spoke.

Yochanan the Immerser (John the Baptist) was the forerunner to Yeshua. Yochanan was very popular with the people. They thought perhaps he was the Messiah. They asked him if he was the one about whom the prophets spoke.

Yochanan said, *".. I am not the Christ (Messiah), but, I have been sent before Him. He who has the bride is the bridegroom; but the friend of the bridegroom, who stands and hears Him, rejoices greatly because of the bridegroom's voice. Therefore this joy of mine is fulfilled"(John 3:28-29).*

The Bride Price

Yochanan introduced Yeshua as the bridegroom, Lamb of God. The bride price Yeshua was willing to pay was His own blood given as the atonement for sin, not only for Israel but also for the Gentiles. Kefa (Peter) wrote, *"knowing that you were not redeemed with corruptible things, like silver or gold, from your aimless conduct received by tradition from your fathers, but with the precious blood of Christ (Messiah), as of a lamb without blemish and without spot"(1 Pet. 1:18-19).*

God came to buy Israel back from her wayward ways with the bride price of His own Son. He was to be the human Lamb of God who would suffer the humiliation spoken of by the prophets, as Hosea was humiliated when he bought his bride.

Isaiah said of Yeshua, *"Surely He has borne our griefs and carried our sorrows; yet we esteemed His stricken, smitten by God, and afflicted. But He was wounded for our transgressions, He was bruised for our iniquities; the chastisement for our peace was upon Him, and by His stripes we are healed. All we like sheep have gone astray; we have turned, every one, to his own way; and the LORD has laid on Him the iniquity of us all"(Is. 53:4-6)*

God chose the bride for His Son. That bride was Israel and all Gentiles who would acknowledge Yeshua as their personal Redeemer.

Yeshua would drink the cup to show He was willing to pay the price. It was the marriage cup of the new covenant at Passover which Yeshua celebrated with His followers.

Mattityahu writes, *"And as they were eating, Jesus (Yeshua) took bread, blessed and broke it, and gave it to the disciples and said, 'Take, eat; for this is My body." Then He took the cup and gave thanks, and gave it to them, saying, 'Drink from it, all of you. For this is My blood of the new covenant, which is shed for many for the remission of sins"(Matt. 26:26-28).*

Yeshua, our divine bridegroom, paid the bride price by the shedding of His own blood. He was the atonement for our sins. He took the curse of our sins on Himself. He was the innocent substitutionary sacrifice who died that we might be reconciled to God.

Isaiah went on to say, *"... For He was cut off from the land of the living; for the transgressions of My people He was stricken. And they made His grave with the wicked, but with the rich at His death, because He had done no violence, nor was any deceit in His mouth.*

"Yet it pleased the LORD to bruise Him; He has put Him to grief. When you make His soul an offering for sin, He shall see His seed, He shall prolong His days, and the pleasure of the LORD shall prosper in His hands"(Is. 53:8-10).

The Bridegroom Resurrected

Isaiah said that Yeshua would prolong His days. This prophecy came true three days after Yeshua was crucified. It was after the Sabbath, in the early morning, when followers of Yeshua went to His tomb to anoint His body. But they were greeted by an angel of the Lord who said to them, "... *Do not be afraid, for I know that you seek Jesus (Yeshua) who was crucified. He is not here; for He is risen, as He said. Come, see the place where the Lord lay"(Matt. 28:5-6).*

Yeshua was resurrected according to the prophets. He then spent forty days with His bride, the Messianic Jews who acknowledged Him as Messiah. Then He said to them, *"In My Father's house are many mansions; if it were not so, I would have told you. I go to prepare a place for you. And if I go and prepare a place for you, I will come again and receive you to Myself; that where I am, there you may be also"(John 14:2-3)*

Yeshua spoke to His disciples like a bridegroom would speak to his bride. He was going to prepare the wedding chamber, the New Jerusalem, which was in heaven. It would be our eternal *chuppah*.

Yochanan wrote, *"Then I, John saw the holy city, New Jerusalem, coming down out of heaven from God, prepared as a bride adorned for her husband"(Rev. 21:2).*

An angel said to Yochanan, *"... Come, I will show you the bride, the Lamb's wife. And he carried me away in the Spirit to a great a high mountain, and he showed me the great city, the holy Jerusalem, descending out of heaven from God"(Rev. 21:9-10).*

What a wedding chamber Yeshua is preparing for His bride. It is illuminated by the glory of God that shines throughout the entire chamber, even penetrating the ceilings, walls, and floors.

Its wall is 216 feet high with twelve gates guarded by twelve angels, who perhaps are the friends of the bridegroom standing outside the wedding chamber to testify to His shed blood. Each gate is made of a single pearl with the names of the twelve tribes written on them.

The foundation of the wedding chamber has twelve layers built upon each other, each layer extending around all four sides of the city. Each layer is made of different precious stones. The names of the twelve apostles of Yeshua are written on the foundation.

The wedding chamber is actually a city approximately 1,500 miles long, 1,500 miles wide and 1,500 miles high. This is over one-half the size of the Unites States mainland and would cover the geographic area from Maine to Florida and the Atlantic Ocean to the Midwestern states. This is the largest wedding chamber that has ever been prepared in the history of mankind.

The entire city, including the streets, is made of pure transparent gold. It is designed to reflect the glory of God in a dazzling display of brilliant color. The glory of God shines throughout the city with a gold cast. This is the true Jerusalem of Gold, the Holy City, the New Jerusalem, the wedding chamber of the bride. (See Rev. 21:9-21).

Once Yeshua prepares the wedding chamber, He will come again for His bride. His followers asked Him, "... *Tell us, when will these things be? And what will be the sign of your coming, and of the end of the age"(Matt. 24:3)?*

Yeshua told them there would be certain signs to tell them His coming is near. But He went on to say, *"But of that day and hour no ones knows, not even the angels of heaven, but My Father only"(Matt. 24:36).*

Since only the Father knows, not the bride nor the Son, we should not be deceived by false prophets and prophecies that pretend to know when He will come for His bride. Like the waiting bride in ancient times, we should know the times and seasons, but not the exact moment He will come.

The Heavenly Matchmaker and the Jews

According to the New Testament, When Yeshua ascended to heaven, He sent the perfect matchmaker, the Ruach-HaKodesh (Holy Spirit) to find all Jews and Gentiles who would become part of His bride. We would be one in Him.

Yeshua said, *"And I will pray the Father, and He will give you another Helper, that He may abide with you forever—the Spirit of truth, whom the world cannot receive, because it neither sees Him nor knows Him; but you know Him, for He dwells with you and will be in you. These things I have spoken to you while being present with you. But the Helper, the Holy Spirit, whom the Father will send in My name, He will teach you all things, and bring to your remembrance all things that I said to you"(John 14:16-17,25-26).*

Yeshua promised to send the Holy Spirit to join us to Himself as a bridegroom and bride are one. The fulfillment of this promise is recorded in the book of Acts. He began with the Jews who were in Jerusalem to celebrate the Feast of Pentecost.

We read these words, *"When the Day of Pentecost had fully come, they were all with one accord in one place. And suddenly there came a sound for heaven, as of a rushing might wind and it filled the whole house where they were sitting. Then there appeared to them divided tongues, as of fire, and one sat upon each of them. And they were all filled with the Holy Spirit and began to speak with other tongues, as the Spirit gave them utterance"(Acts 2:1-4).*

Although many thousands of Jews acknowledged Yeshua as Messiah, the religious leaders who were in power rejected Him for the nation. Yeshua spoke of this rejection in terms of the marriage feast. He said, *"And I say to you that many will come from east and west, and sit down with Abraham, Isaac and Jacob in the kingdom of*

God. But the sons of the kingdom will be cast out into outer darkness. There will be weeping and gnashing of teeth"(Matt, 8:11).

Yeshua also told a parable about a wedding feast to illustrate the same point. He said a king arranged a marriage for his son and sent out special invitations to many to come to the wedding. But they were too busy to come and even persecuted and killed the servants who called them to the feast.

The king destroyed the ungrateful ones and invited others to the wedding who were not really acceptable to him. The wedding hall was filled with guests, but one was not properly dressed in a wedding garment. The king removed the man from the celebration. (See Matthew 22:1-13).

God called the Jewish people to be His bride but only a remnant accepted His invitation. The others did not take the wedding garment of salvation and robe of righteousness offered by Yeshua. Yet, as we learned earlier, God promised that at the end of the age He would woo back His ancient bride and join the Gentiles to them. Together, they would be His glorious bride.

God spoke the following words to the Jewish people through Jeremiah " *'Return, O backsliding children' says the LORD; 'for I am married to you. I will take you, one from a city and two from a family, and I will bring you back to Zion' "Jer. 3:14).*

God promised to bring the Jewish people back to their ancient land and draw them back to Himself. When they are back in the land, they will make themselves ready, and He will come. Psalm 102 tells us, *"You will arise and have mercy on Zion; for the time to favor her, yes, the set time has come. For your servants take pleasure in her stones, and show favor to her dust. So the nations shall fear the name of the LORD, and all the kings of the earth Your glory. For the LORD shall build up Zion; He shall appear in His glory"(Ps. 102:13-16).*

Rabbi Shaul (the apostle Paul) wrote of this time and said, *"For I do not desire, brethren, that you should be ignorant of this mystery, lest you should be wise in your own opinion, that blindness in part has happened to Israel until the fullness of the Gentiles has come in. And so all Israel will be saved, as it is written: 'The Deliverer will come out of Zion, and He will turn away ungodliness from Jacob; for this is My covenant with them, when I take away their sins' "(Rom. 11:26-27).*

Today, four million Jews are back in their land. Soon the six million from America will go to Israel as well as the remaining one million in the former Soviet Union. The Jews from the rest of the nations will also return to their ancient land. At the same time this is happening, more and more Jews are acknowledging Yeshua as the Messiah. In fact, there are more Jews today who believe that Yeshua is the Messiah than in the last two thousand years. This number is growing as God is preparing His Messianic bride.

If we have ears to hear, we can hear God calling to His ancient bride, "Return O' Israel. Return to your land.

Return to your God. You left Me, but I have never left you. I have loved you with an everlasting love. I have been waiting for you for a long time.

"I have prepared a place for you, and I am coming soon. Leave the nations and return to your land and your God. I am even now judging the nations because of their wickedness and their hatred of you. But My plans for you are different.

"I am calling you to My banqueting table, and I will not rest to you come to Me and Jerusalem is a praise on the earth.

"For I have set My eyes on you for good, and I will bring you back to your land. I will build you up and not pull you down. I will plant you and not pluck you up. I will give you a heart to know Me, that I am the LORD. You shall be My bride, and I will be your husband God for you shall return to Me with all your heart.

"For I know the thoughts that I think toward you. Thoughts of peace and not of evil, to give you a future and a hope. Then you will call upon Me and go and pray to Me, and I will listen to you. And you will seek Me and find Me, when you search for Me with all your heart.

"I will be found by you, and I will bring you back from your captivity; I will gather you from all the nations and from all the places where I have driven you. I will bring you to the place from which I caused you to be carried away captive.

"Yes, I will cause you to return and rebuild those places as at the first. I will cleanse you from all your iniquity by which you have sinned against Me. I will pardon all your iniquities to be remembered no more.

"Again there shall be heard in the land which had been desolate the voice of joy and the voice of gladness, the voice of the bridegroom and the voice of the bride, the voice of those who will say: 'Praise the LORD of hosts, for the LORD is good, for His mercy endures forever.' "

The Heavenly Matchmaker and the Gentiles

Yeshua sent the same Holy Spirit upon the Gentiles as God promised He would by the prophets. Joel wrote, *"And it shall come to pass afterward that I will pour My Spirit on all flesh; your sons and your daughters shall prophesy, your old men shall dream dreams, your young men shall see visions. And also on My menservants and on My maidservants I will pour out My Spirit in those days" (Joel 2:28-29).*

This initial fulfillment of this event is also recorded in the book of Acts when God sent the Holy Spirit upon a man named Cornelius and his family and friends. God had instructed Kefa (Peter) to go and preach to this man. When Kefa told them about Yeshua, the Spirit of God fell on them all. We read, *"While Peter was still speaking these words, the Holy Spirit fell upon all those who heard the word. And those of the circumcision (Jews) who believed were astonished, as many as came with Peter, because the gift of the Holy Spirit had been poured out on the Gentiles also (Acts 10:44-45).*

Shaul considered the church to be the bride of Messiah (Eph. 5:22-32). He said, *"For I am jealous for you with godly jealousy. For I have betrothed you to one husband, that I may present you as a chaste virgin to Christ (Messiah)"(2 Cor. 11:2).*

But he did not think that God is a bigamist. God doesn't have two brides, one Jew and the other Gentile. Neither did he believe that the church had replaced Israel as God's bride.

Shaul taught that the Gentiles could become God's bride by embracing Yeshua and the new covenant. In this way, Gentiles would be joined to the original bride, Israel.

Messianic Jews would not become part of the bride by joining the Gentile church. To the contrary, Gentile believers would become part of the bride by joining themselves to the Messianic community. (See Romans 11).

You see, God does not intend for the church to replace natural Israel as God's bride. Instead, Gentile believers are joined to Jewish believers through Messiah.

Through Yeshua, both Jew and Gentile can be God's bride. Shaul wrote, *"There is neither Jew nor Greek, there is neither slave nor free, there is neither male nor female; for you are all one in Christ Jesus (Messiah Yeshua) (Gal. 3:28).*

Paul did not mean there would no longer be a ethnic distinction between Jew and Gentile but that we can be one in Messiah Yeshua. The Holy Spirit would choose the bride for Yeshua from both Jews and Gentiles and make them one bride.

Making Ourselves Ready

When we accept the marriage contract offered to us by Yeshua, we drink the cup of acceptance. That cup is the new covenant meal of communion. It represents our union with Him. We are in Him and He is in us. The two of us have become one.

Shaul wrote, *"For I received from the Lord that which I also delivered to you: that the Lord Jesus on the same night in which He was betrayed took bread; and when He had given thanks, He broke it and said, 'Take, eat; this is My body which is broken for you; do this in remembrance of Me.' In the same manner He also took the cup after supper, saying, 'This cup is the new covenant in My blood. This do in remembrance of Me.' For as often as you eat this bread and drink this cup, you proclaim the Lord's death till He comes"(1 Cor. 11:23-26).*

When we become Yeshua's bride, we partake of the mikveh of baptism. Peter preached to the Jews, *"Repent, and let every one of you be baptized in the name of Jesus Christ (Yeshua Messiah) for the remission of sins, and you shall receive the gift of the Holy Spirit"(Acts 2:38).* Likewise, Peter instructed the Gentiles to be baptized, *"And he commanded them to be baptized in the name of the Lord"(Acts 10:48).*

Yeshua has also given gifts to His bride so that we might make ourselves beautiful for Him. These are listed for us in 1 Corinthians 12, Romans 12 and Ephesians 4:11). We are to use these gifts for God's glory and the benefit of

His bride. As Peter wrote, *"As each one has received a gift, minister it to one another as good stewards of the manifold grace of God"(1 Pet. 4:10).*

Yeshua said He would come again for His bride. Until that time, we are to make ourselves ready. John wrote, " *'Let us be glad and rejoice and give Him glory, for the marriage of the Lamb has come, and His wife has made herself ready.' And to her it was granted to be arrayed in fine linen, clean and bright, for the fine linen is the righteous acts of the saints"(Rev. 19:7-8).*

Through Yeshua, Messianic Jews and righteous Gentiles are God's special treasure. We are His purchased possession (Eph. 1:14). We have been bought with a price and are to glorify Him in our body and spirit which belong to Him (1 Cor. 6:14).

We are not to love the world neither the things that are in the world (1 Jn. 2:15). We are to be holy as He is holy (1 Pet. 1:15-16). We are to keep ourselves for Him for He is jealous over us (James 4:5). We are His "me'kudeshet." Our one passion should be a longing to see our heavenly bridegroom face to face and enter into the wedding chamber with Him.

Although we do not know exactly when Yeshua will come, we must be ready at all times. Yeshua told a parable about ten virgins who took their lamps and went out to meet the bridegroom. Five were wise virgins who took oil for their lamps. Five were foolish who had no oil for their lamps. When the bridegroom was delayed, they fell asleep. Finally, at midnight the cry was heard that the bridegroom was coming. But the foolish virgins lamps went out and they had no oil to light them and were not able to attend the wedding.

Yeshua used this story to warn us to be ready for His coming. (See Matthew 25:1-13). He said, *"Watch therefore, for you know neither the day nor the hour in which the Son of Man is coming"(Matt. 25:13).*

As the approaching bridegroom gave a shout and blew the shofar to alert his bride, so Yeshua will also come for us. He is anxious to come for us, but wants us to be ready.

Paul writes, *"For the Lord Himself will descend from heaven with a shout, with the voice of an archangel, and with the trumpet of God. And the dead in Christ (Messiah) will rise first. Then we who are alive and remain shall be caught up together with them in the clouds to meet the Lord in the air. And thus we shall always be with the Lord.*

"Therefore comfort one another with these words. But concerning the times and the seasons, brethren, you have no need that I should write to you. For you yourselves know perfectly that the day of the Lord so comes as a thief in the night"(1 Thess. 4:16-5:1)

The Marriage Feast

Finally, God's bride will have a joyous marriage feast on the earth. It's called the millennium because it will last one thousand years. An angel in the book of Revelation said to John, "... *Blessed are those who are called to the marriage supper of the Lamb ... ."(Rev. 19:9).*

We will be celebrating our glorious marriage to the King of Kings and Lord of Lords. We will reign with Him as His bride on the earth.

As God is calling the Messianic part of His bride back to Himself, He is doing the same to the Gentiles.

When the Berlin wall and the iron curtain of communism fell, Eastern Europe and Russia opened up to the Gospel of Yeshua. Millions of these former athiest are now becoming part of the bride of Yeshua. Soon China and Japan will do the same. Hundreds of millions of Chinese and tens of millions of Japanese will become part of the bride.

Millions in the West will also soon cry out to God for redemption as He reveals His glory throughout the earth. The greatest outpouring of the Ruach-HaKodesh the world has ever know will soon take place as God is completing the fullness of the Gentiles and preparing His bride.

God is calling the Gentiles throughout the world to Himself. As with the Jews, if we listen closely we can hear Him say, "Come away My beloved. I have called you to Myself. There is nothing this world can offer that can satisfy you. I alone can meet your every need and fulfill the deepest longings of your heart for love and companionship

"The end of all things is at hand. The world as you know it will soon pass away. The kingdoms of this world will soon perish. Come out of it and be separate. Turn from your wicked ways, your lukewarmness, you lack of love. Draw near to Me, and I will draw near to you.

"Set your affections on things that are above. Seek first My kingdom and My righteousness. Flee temptation. Resist the Devil. Trim your wicks! Fill your lamps with oil! Put on your wedding garment! Make yourself ready for I am coming soon.

"Difficult times are at hand. But don't be afraid. For I have prepared a place for you. It is almost complete. I am coming soon to take you to Myself that where I am you may be also. It is a place filled with My glory. I want to share it with you. I want to know you and be known by you.

"My wedding garment for you is without spot or blemish. You will wear it in our wedding chamber. There you will have joy unspeakable and full of glory. You will look upon Me as I am, face to face, for you shall be like Me. Your heart will find contentment resting in My arms of love.

"Nothing shall separate you from Me. No, not death, not life, nor angels nor principalities nor powers, nor things present nor things to come, nor height nor depth, nor any other creature shall be able to separate you from my love. Look up for your redemption draws near."

Until He comes, our holy lives are the veils that separate us from the world. We are in the world but not of the world. We belong to Yeshua. We keep ourselves pure for Him.

Although the world may not recognize us today as the bride of Yeshua, they will when we appear with Him at His coming for we shall be like Him (Phil. 3:20-21).

When we appear with Him as His unveiled bride, the whole world will know who we are and proclaim, **"Here comes the bride."**

About the Author

Richard Booker is a Bible teacher and author known for his ability to communicate difficult subjects in an easy-to-understand manner. He has written many books which have touched the lives of people around the world.

In 1974, God dramatically changed Richard's life while he was studying the book of Leviticus. *He saw Jesus in every book of the Bible.* Afterwards, Richard left his successful business career to teach and write about the insights God was giving him.

A list of some of Richard's books and tapes on the "Jewish Roots of Christianity" is provided on the following pages. *If you would like a catalog describing all of his books and teaching materials contact him and request a Ministry Catalog.*

Richard, along with his wife, Peggy, travel extensively sharing God's Word with clarity and love to both believing Gentiles and Jews. If you would like Richard to come to your *church*, *congregation* or *conference* to teach and minister, contact him at his Houston address.

Richard and Peggy take *tour groups to Israel* each year where Richard is a regular speaker at the International Christian Celebration of the Feast of Tabernacles. These are comprehensive quality tours where you travel the land of the Bible and participate in the festive activities of the Feast. *Write for tour information.*

BOOK AND TAPE CATALOG

Here Comes the Bride

One of the most beautiful pictures of God's love is the ancient Jewish wedding. This book explains *Jewish wedding customs* and how they point to the Messiah as well as what we can do to prepare ourselves for the greatest event of the ages, the wedding of God's bride.

Blow the Trumpet in Zion

This book explains the dramatic and fascinating story of the Jewish people, Israel and the nations in prophecy. It is *one of the most informative books available* relating Bible prophecy to world history and current and future events as they revolve around God's covenant plan for the Jewish people and Israel.

Jesus in the Feasts of Israel

This is a study of the Old Testament feasts showing how they pointed to Jesus and their *personal* and *prophetic* significance for today's world. The reader also discovers how the feasts represents seven steps in the believer's walk with God.

How the Cross Became a Sword

This publication explains the events that separated Christianity from its Jewish roots and established anti-Semitism as official church doctrine. It then gives an *excellent overview* of the tragic history of Christian-Jewish relations directly linking modern replacement theology to the first Christian seminary in Alexandria, Egypt.

Islam, Christianity and Israel

This publication reveals shocking information about the life of Mohammed and the background, teachings and practices of Islam. It also explains how Islam differs from Christianity and is threatening to conquer the West. The reader learns "*what they won't tell you on the evening news*" about the conflict between the Arabs and the Jews and how the conflict will end.

BOOK ORDER FORM

To order books on Jewish-Christian studies, check the appropriate box, then clip and mail the coupon below to: Sounds of the Trumpet, 4747 Research Forest Drive, Suite 180-330, The Woodlands, Texas 77381, www.rbooker.com

❑ Please send me ____ copy(ies) of *Here Comes the Bride*. I have enclosed $7.95 for each book ordered (includes shipping).

❑ Please send me ____ copy(ies) of *Blow the Trumpet in Zion*. I have enclosed $12.00 for each book ordered (includes shipping).

❑ Please send me ____ copy(ies) of *Jesus in the Feasts of Israel*. I have enclosed $12.00 for each book ordered (includes shipping).

❑ Please send me ____ copy(ies) of *How the Cross Became A Sword*. I have enclosed $7.95 for each book ordered (includes shipping).

❑ Please send me ____ copy(ies) of *Islam, Christianity and Israel*. I have enclosed $7.95 for each book ordered (includes shipping).

- -

Name ______________________________
Address ____________________________
City _______________________________
State ______________ Zip ____________

Foreign orders please send an additional $2.00 per book ordered in U.S. funds only for surface mail.

TAPE ORDER FORM

To order tapes on Jewish-Christian studies, check the appropriate box, then clip and mail the coupon below to: Sounds of the Trumpet, 4747 Research Forest Drive, Ste. 180-330, The Woodlands, TX 77381,www.rbooker.com

All tapes are $5.00 each (includes shipping). Please enclose payment with order. Foreign orders please add an additional $2.00 per tape ordered in U.S. dollars only for surface mail.

- ❑ Why God Chose the Jews
- ❑ Israel and Nations in Prophecy
- ❑ Time to Favor Zion
- ❑ Times of the Gentiles
- ❑ The Messianic Kingdom
- ❑ How the Cross Became A Sword
- ❑ Islam, Christianity and Israel
- ❑ How to Recognize the Jewish Messiah
- ❑ Israel or Palestine: Whose Land is it?
- ❑ Expressing Christian Love to the Jews
- ❑ Survey of the Feasts
- ❑ Celebrating the Feasts in the Church

Name ______________________________

Address ____________________________

City _______________________________

State _______________ Zip _______________